HAL LEONARD

VOCAL METHOD

dition

Introduction 2

How to use this book 2

PREPARATION 3

   Posture 3

   Physical Warm-up 3

   Breath 3

   Using the Breath 4

   Phonation 4

   Warmups 4

   Vowels 5

   Consonants 5

SONGS 6

   Can't Help Falling in Love. 6

   Stand By Me 10

   Take Me Home, Country Roads. 15

   Fly Me to the Moon 20

   Hallelujah 25

   Fields of Gold 29

   Fire and Rain 33

   Mad World 38

   Haven't Met You Yet. 42

   Perfect 49

   Yesterday 54

   Crazy Little Thing Called Love 59

PLAYBACK+
Speed • Pitch • Balance • Loop

To access audio and video visit:
www.halleonard.com/mylibrary

Enter Code
3906-5574-7588-7448

ISBN 978-1-70510-760-7

HAL•LEONARD®

Visit Hal Leonard Online at
www.halleonard.com

Contact us:
Hal Leonard
7777 West Bluemound Road
Milwaukee, WI 53213
Email: info@halleonard.com

In Europe, contact:
Hal Leonard Europe Limited
42 Wigmore Street
Marylebone, London, W1U 2RN
Email: info@halleonardeurope.com

In Australia, contact:
Hal Leonard Australia Pty. Ltd.
4 Lentara Court
Cheltenham, Victoria, 3192 Australia
Email: info@halleonard.com.au

INTRODUCTION

Congratulations! If you are reading this then you are thinking about becoming a better singer. Our goal is to help you by providing both techniques and songs that will lead you to success.

If you take a moment to think about what makes a singer "popular," you will realize that it's not necessarily about having the "greatest" voice but rather the most "unique" and recognizable instrument AND the ability to tell a good story through song.

Of course, singing in tune and with musicality is a major part of the equation, but the goal here is to further your "unique" instrument and provide positive reinforcement and concepts that will make you more effective and confident when you perform. I guarantee that if you will follow the advice in this book, those goals will be met and your enjoyment of singing enhanced.

Best wishes,
Roger Emerson

HOW TO USE THIS BOOK

The book is divided into two sections: PREPARATION and SONGS. We have included both lyric sheets and notation. If you would like to learn more about notation, please check out "Sight Singing Made Simple" by David Bauguess (HL47819111).

You may be tempted to jump right to the songs, but I encourage you start with the Preparation section. Like a good athlete, warming up and skill exercises are important before you start playing. The same can be said for successful singing!

The songs are generally sequenced with the easiest at the beginning and the more challenging towards the end, but feel free to jump around and sing those songs that motivate you the most, first. A variety of styles have been provided for your enjoyment and growth. The songs are presented in a variety of keys. Some will fit the lower (bass) voice, while others the higher (tenor) voice. Having said that, don't lock yourself into any one vocal classification. The goal should always be to sing the widest range possible. Also, this book features the *PLAYBACK+* feature which allows you to change the key up or down to better fit your comfort range. You can also speed up or slow down the song as desired for practice or performance.

Finally, each song will have suggestions for effective performance provided. Often the suggestion will apply to other songs in the book as well. Remember, these are only ideas. Singing is an art, and you should make the song your own and provide your own treatment. Effective communication of the lyric (telling the story) is the ultimate goal. Let's begin!

POSTURE ▶

As with any "method" book, holding the instrument is a good starting point. Realize that your voice IS a true instrument. It may not have buttons or strings, but it does have all the components of a typical musical instrument, i.e., a method of propulsion (air), a sound generator (the vocal cords) and a resonator (your mouth and face).

EXERCISE 1:

- Stand Tall.

- Feet spaced evenly with your shoulders.

- Strong foot slightly ahead of the other.

- Arms relaxed at your sides.

- Rib cage elevated but not rigid.

As a singer you most likely will move somewhat when singing, particularly if you are using a hand-held microphone. One hand may hold the mic while the other is used for expression. If the mic is on a stand you may use both hands for expression. Be careful not to overdo motion. It is better to "bring the audience to you," with the face being the main means of communication.

PHYSICAL WARM-UP ▶

Because we sing with our "entire body," it's a good idea to do a few stretches before we sing.

These are like any physical warmup you would do before an athletic event.

EXERCISE 2:

Do each several times.

- Raise your hands over your head and reach high.

- Wave arms left and right.

- Bring arms down to side and shake them out.

- Roll your shoulders forward, backward, up and down.

- Allow chin to drop to chest and then backward, left and right.

- Hands on hips and rock pelvis forward and back.

- March in place.

- Relax and assume singing posture as described above (stand tall, etc.)

BREATH ▶

Proper breath support and airstream cannot occur effectively if the elements of "posture" outlined above are not employed. Standing tall with the rib cage elevated allows you to breathe fully. It is also important to realize the we sing with our "entire body," from our feet to the top of our head.

If room allows, lie on your back. Begin by exhaling all of the air in your lungs then inhale to a slow eight counts (about eight seconds). You may breathe through your nose, mouth or some combination as most singers do. Sense the expansion that occurs around your mid-section. Now exhale for eight counts through pursed lips as if you are going to whistle but make no sound. This sensation of a "full breath" and controlled exhalation "air stream" are VERY important to successful vocal production. Repeat this exercise four times.

USING THE BREATH

Since air is such an important part of a vibrant vocal sound, don't skimp on these exercises and make sure that the "sensation" of a full breath and controlled exhalation is a conscious part of "singing" each phrase of every song you sing. **Let me repeat: Remember to take a full breath before every phrase that you sing and then use the air to propel the phrase!**

EXERCISE 3:

- With singing posture in place, breathe in low and deep to a slow eight counts. (Remember the sensation should be the same as when you were lying flat.)

- Now hiss the air out (exhale) for a slow eight counts. (Repeat four times.)

- Breathe in low and deep to a slow 12 counts. Feel the sensation of expansion around your navel and back. DO NOT let shoulders heave up and down. The upper body remains relaxed and the rib cage elevated but not rigid.

- Hiss the air out for a slow 12 counts. Notice how once you have exhaled fully, air will naturally flow back into the lungs. (Repeat four times.)

- Breathe in quickly to four counts and do a relaxed sigh from high to low. (Repeat 4 times.)

PHONATION – MAKING A SOUND

You are now ready to sing! In fact, you just did when you "sighed" from high to low in the last exercise. Singing is nothing more than a "sustained sigh."

Try this: Breathe in (inhale) to a quick 4-count, sigh from high to low but halfway down, hold that pitch and continue the sound until the breath is fully exhaled. If posture is in place, and you've taken a full, low breath, the result should be a full and vibrant sound.

If you are like most people, you probably sighed on an "ah" like a yawn in the morning. That is good and natural. Now try this:

Sigh from high to low with your lips closed to a hum. Midway down, open to an "ah."

Repeat four times.

Let's experiment by stopping at various points from high to low and going from a "hum" to an "ah." Don't forget to inhale fully and let the exhalation do the work! If you find yourself forcing the sound, go back to that "morning sigh."

LET'S USE ALL THAT WE HAVE LEARNED!

If you are not familiar with musical notation, please check out "Sight Singing Made Simple" by David Bauguess (HL47819111).

WARMUP #1

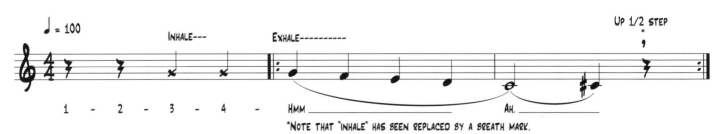

*"NOTE THAT "INHALE" HAS BEEN REPLACED BY A BREATH MARK.

Let's do a variation of the same warmup.

WARMUP #2 ▶

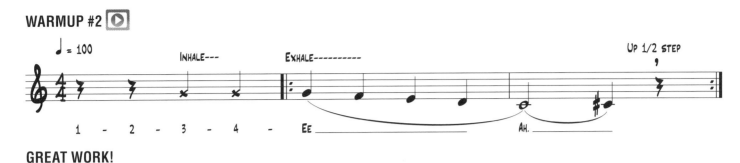

GREAT WORK!

VOWELS

Space inside the mouth will create a richer sounding singing voice. An easy way to "feel" this space is by imagining what you do when you eat something very hot and try not to burn the inside of your mouth.

You have probably heard the term "tall vowels." Simply stated a "tall vowel" is an ah, oh, oo, ee or eh sound that is sung with the jaw lowered, and the the soft pallet at the back of the throat raised, (like you do when you eat something hot!). The lips are also slightly pursed on all but the "ah" vowel.

If you put your fingers to the jaw hinge adjacent to your ear and open wide, you will feel a space created. Classical singers use VERY tall vowels, the pop singer not so much as popular music does not require nearly as much resonance but it is still important to recognize these five vowel sounds which occur within the lyrics of a song. These vowel shapes can be emphasized on long sounds to make the voice sound better. Let's refer to them as "warm vowels."

Here is an exercise to practice these vowel shapes:

WARMUP #3 ▶

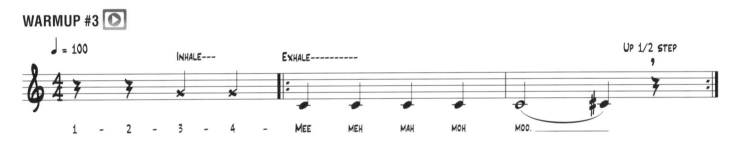

CONSONANTS

Consonants (t,p,m,n,c, etc.) provide clarity and energy to your singing. A simple exercise is to quickly repeat the phrase: "The lips, the teeth, the tip of the tongue!"

WARMUP #4 ▶

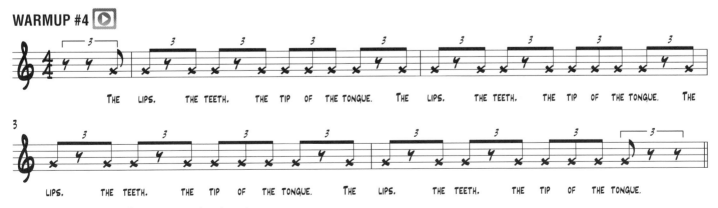

For more great vocal warmups check out:
Vocal Warm-Ups – HL00740395
Vocal Exercises – HL00123770

LET'S SING!

CAN'T HELP FALLING IN LOVE

FUN FACTS:

"Can't Help Falling in Love" is a 1961 song recorded by American singer Elvis Presley. It has been recorded (covered) multiple times by many artists, most recently Twenty One Pilots in a version that featured ukulele accompaniment. The song was initially written for a woman as "Can't Help Falling in Love with Him" which explains the first and third line ending on "in" and "sin" rather than words rhyming with "you."

PERFORMANCE TIPS:

Ballads (slow songs) offer a unique opportunity to explore phrasing. A phrase is merely a musical sentence such as "Wise men say only fools rush in." This one thought can be sung two ways depending upon the speed of the song: all on one breath or broken into two shorter phrases. Elvis chose to perform the piece quite slowly and hence breaks the phrase in the middle. Either way, there should be a slight crescendo (get louder) in the middle of the phrase and then decrescendo (get softer) towards the end. Below are two ways to interpret the song.

EXAMPLE 1: SHORT PHRASES

EXAMPLE 2: LONG PHRASE

More songs like this can be found in *Music Minus One: Elvis Presley* (HL00279891)

CAN'T HELP FALLING IN LOVE

Wise men say only fools rush in,

But I can't help falling in love with you.

Shall I stay? Would it be a sin

If I can't help falling in love with you?

Like a river flows surely to the sea,

Darling, so it goes, some things are meant to be.

Take my hand, take my whole life too.

For I can't help falling in love with you.

Like a river flows surely to the sea,

Darling, so it goes, some things are meant to be.

Take my hand, take my whole life too.

For I can't help falling in love with you.

For I can't help falling in love with you.

CAN'T HELP FALLING IN LOVE

Words and Music by George David Weiss,
Hugo Peretti and Luigi Creatore

19 F#m ... C#7 ... F#m ... C#7

LIKE A ___ RIV - ER FLOWS ___ SURE - LY ___ TO THE SEA. ___

21 F#m ... C#7 ... F#m ... B9sus2

DAR - LING. ___ SO IT GOES. ___ SOME THINGS ___ ARE ___ MEANT TO

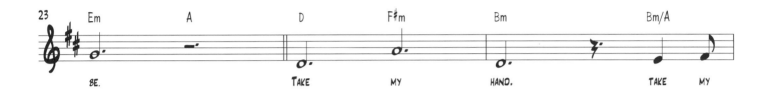

23 Em ... A ... D ... F#m ... Bm ... Bm/A

BE. ___ TAKE MY HAND. ___ TAKE MY

26 G ... D/F# ... A/E ... A ... G ... A

WHOLE LIFE TOO. ___ FOR I CAN'T

29 Bm ... Em ... D/A ... A ... 1. D ... D/A

HELP ___ FALL - ING ___ IN ___ LOVE ___ WITH YOU.

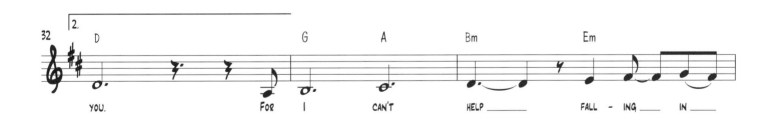

2. 32 D ... G ... A ... Bm ... Em

YOU. ___ FOR I CAN'T HELP ___ FALL - ING ___ IN ___

SLOWER

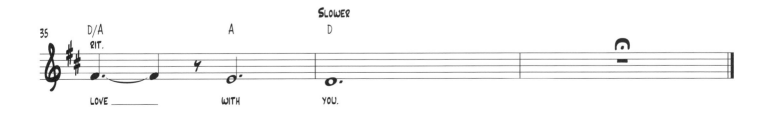

35 D/A ... A ... D

RIT.

LOVE ___ WITH YOU.

STAND BY ME

FUN FACT:

"Stand by Me" began as a spiritual written by Same Cooke and J.W. Alexander called "Stand by Me Father." The song takes on a whole new meaning when considered in this light.

PERFORMANCE TIPS:

This song is a perfect example of the impact of space or silence when singing. Notice the contrast between measures 1-4 and measures 5-7 below. It has been said that rests (silence) are the windows of music. As you learn and perform new songs, look for opportunities to apply this principle.

EXAMPLE 1:

More songs like this can be found in *Hits of the '60's* Pro Vocal, Volume 36 (HL00740382).

STAND BY ME

When the night has come

And the land is dark

And the moon is the only light we'll see.

No I won't be afraid,

No I won't be afraid

Just as long as you stand, stand by me.

So darlin', darlin', stand by me,

Whoa, stand by me.

Oh, stand, stand by me, stand by me.

If the sky that we look upon

Should tumble and fall,

Or the mountain should crumble to the sea.

I won't cry, I won't cry,

No, I won't shed a tear

Just as long as you stand, stand by me.

So darlin', darlin' stand by me,

Whoa stand by me.

Oh, stand, stand by me, stand by me.

So darlin', darlin', stand by me,

Whoa stand by me.

Oh, stand, stand by me, stand by me.

So darlin', darlin', stand by me,

Whoa, stand by me.

Oh, stand, stand by me, stand by me.

Oh, stand, stand by me, stand by me.

Oh, stand, stand by me, stand by me.

STAND BY ME

Words and Music by Jerry Leiber,
Mike Stoller and Ben E. King

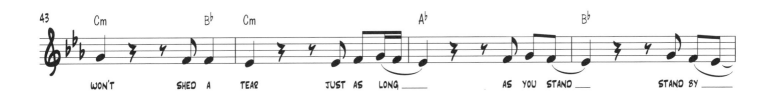

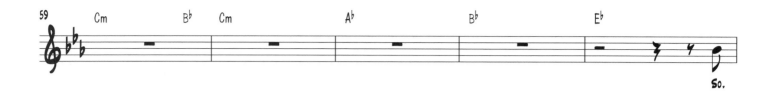

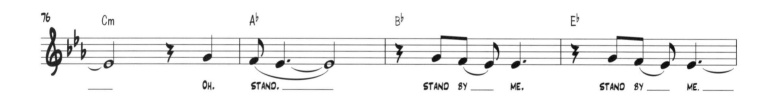

TAKE ME HOME, COUNTRY ROADS

FUN FACTS:

"Take Me Home, Country Roads" was originally intended for Johnny Cash, however when John Denver heard it he told the writers, "I must have it!" Denver then helped re-write the song and add a bridge. It was originally going to be about Massachusetts instead of West Virginia (both have 4 syllables) but they decided that the latter was more picturesque. The song has more recently been featured in the video game "Fallout 76."

PERFORMANCE TIPS: ▶

As with many country artists and songs, the vocal tone used is brighter. We call this "singing in the mask" as the tone is placed more in the front of the mouth. Also, with this song the short phrases on the verse lend themselves to "talking" the notes a bit instead of sustaining them as you do on the chorus.

Our voice has many tone colors, but most often we refer to them as "dark" or "bright." To practice this, sing an "ah" deep in the back of the throat and gradually move it forward to the front of the teeth then back again. I use a scale of 1 to 10, with 1 being the darkest and 10 being the brightest. This song can be sung on about an 8. You may also want to use "warm vowels" on the chorus for words like "roads" and "home."

EXAMPLE 1:

More Songs like this can be found in *Neil Diamond* Pro Vocal, Volume 40 (HL00740387).

TAKE ME HOME, COUNTRY ROADS

Almost heaven, West Virginia,

Blue Ridge Mountains, Shenandoah River.

Life was old there, older than the trees,

Younger than the mountains blowing like a breeze.

Country roads, take me home

To the place I belong:

West Virginia, Mountain Momma,

Take me home, country roads.

All my mem'ries gather 'round her,

Miner's lady, stranger to blue water

Dark and dusty, painted on the sky,

Misty taste of moonshine, teardrops in my eye.

Country roads, take me home

To the place I belong:

West Virginia, Mountain Momma,

Take me home, country roads.

I hear her voice in the mornin' hour she calls me.

The radio reminds me of my home far away.

And drivin' down the road I get a feelin'

That I shoud-a been home yesterday, yesterday.

Country roads, take me home

To the place I belong:

West Virginia, Mountain Momma

Take me home, country roads.

Why don't you take me home, country roads.

Why don't you take me home, country roads.

Take me home, country roads.

Why don't you take me home, country roads.

TAKE ME HOME, COUNTRY ROADS

Words and Music by John Denver,
Bill Danoff and Taffy Nivert

WEST VIR - GIN - IA, _____ MOUN - TAIN MOM - MA, _____

TAKE ____ ME HOME. COUN - TRY ROADS.

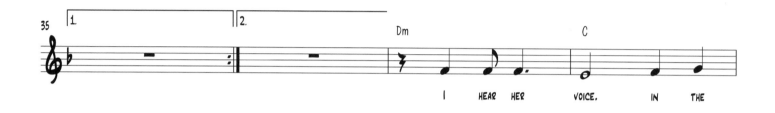

1. 2. I HEAR HER VOICE, IN THE

MORN - IN' HOUR SHE CALLS ____ ME. THE RA - DI - O ____ RE - MINDS ____ ME OF MY

HOME FAR A - WAY. ____ AND DRIV - IN' DOWN THE ROAD ____ I GET A

FEEL - IN' THAT I SHOULD - A BEEN HOME YES - TER - DAY. ____ YES - TER - DAY. _

_____ COUN - TRY ROADS, TAKE ____ ME HOME

TO THE PLACE ___ I BE - LONG: ___ WEST VIR - GIN -

- IA, ___ MOUN - TAIN MOM - MA. ___ TAKE ___ ME

HOME. COUN - TRY ROADS. WHY DON'T YOU TAKE ___ ME

HOME. COUN - TRY ROADS. WHY DON'T YOU TAKE ___ ME

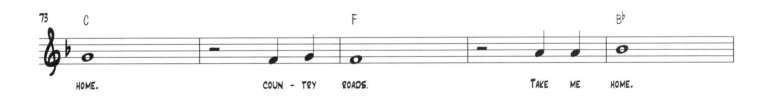

HOME. COUN - TRY ROADS. TAKE ME HOME.

COUN - TRY ROADS. WHY DON'T YOU TAKE ___ ME HOME. ___

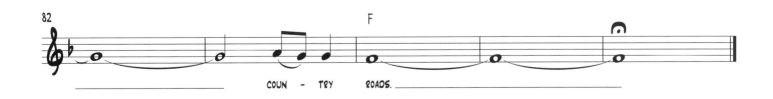

___ COUN - TRY ROADS. ___

FLY ME TO THE MOON

FUN FACTS:

"Fly Me to the Moon" was originally written in waltz time (3/4), with an accent every three beats instead of every four, which gave it a "lilting" bounce. It is rarely performed that way anymore, now usually performed in a straight ahead 4/4 swing feel. The best example is any recording by Frank Sinatra. Use it as a guide for your performance.

PERFORMANCE TIPS: ▶

A hallmark of songs performed in a "swing" style is that they are sung "conversationally" and relaxed. And when we say a song "swings," what we really mean is that the eighth notes are treated unevenly as part of a triplet, instead of evenly as you would find in most pop and rock songs. Listen to the two examples below which demonstrate the difference.

EXAMPLE 1: STRAIGHT

EXAMPLE 2: SWING

More songs like this can be found in *Jazz Standards* Pro Vocal, Volume 2 (HL00740250).

FLY ME TO THE MOON

Fly me to the moon,

And let me play among the stars.

Let me see what spring is like on

Jupiter and Mars.

In other words, hold my hand.

In other words, baby, kiss me.

Fill my heart with song,

And let me sing forevermore.

You are all I long for,

All I worship and adore.

In other words, please be true.

In other words, I love you.

Fill my heart with song,

Let me sing forevermore.

You are all I long for,

All I worship and adore.

In other words, please be true.

In other words, in other words, I love you.

FLY ME TO THE MOON

Words and Music by
Bart Howard

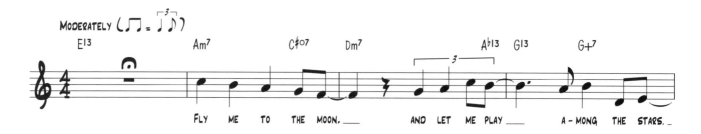

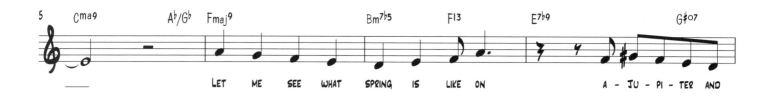

20 | G13 | G+7 | Cma9 | A♭/G♭ Fmaj9 | Bm7♭5 | F13

___ FOR - EV - ER - MORE. YOU ARE ALL I LONG ___ FOR, ALL I

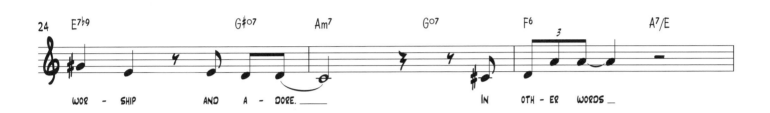

24 | E7♭9 | G#°7 Am7 | G°7 | F6 | A7/E

WOR - SHIP AND A - DORE. ___ IN OTH - ER WORDS ___

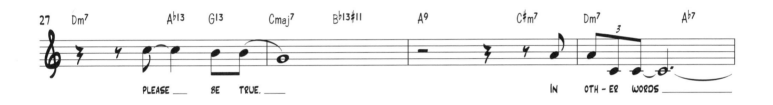

27 | Dm7 | A♭13 G13 Cmaj7 | B♭13#11 A9 | C#m7 Dm7 | A♭7

PLEASE ___ BE TRUE. ___ IN OTH - ER WORDS ___

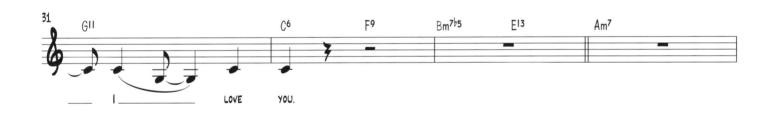

31 | G11 | C6 | F9 | Bm7♭5 E13 | Am7

___ I ___ LOVE YOU.

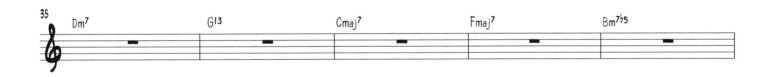

35 | Dm7 | G13 | Cmaj7 | Fmaj7 | Bm7♭5

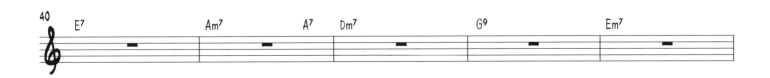

40 | E7 | Am7 | A7 Dm7 | G9 | Em7

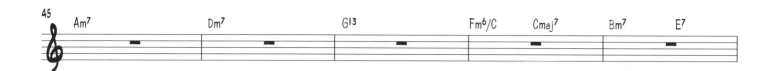

FILL MY HEART WITH SONG, ___ LET ME SING ___ FOR - EV - ER - MORE. ___

___ YOU ARE ALL I LONG FOR, ALL I WOR - SHIP AND A - DORE. ___

IN OTH - ER WORDS. ___ PLEASE ___ BE TRUE. ___

___ IN OTH - ER WORDS. ___ IN OTH - ER WORDS. ___

___ I LOVE YOU.

HALLELUJAH

FUN FACTS:

Leonard Cohen actually wrote over 100 verses to "Hallelujah," reflecting his feelings and thoughts over many years. This published version features the most often heard and officially published ones.

PERFORMANCE TIPS:

Lyrics are always important. However, when telling a story – as Cohen was famous for – they are even more critical. In order to give impact to any lyric, pick out the most important words in each phrase and give them added emphasis. There is no right or wrong way to do this. Listen to the two examples below, which emphasize different words in the identical lyric.

Also keep in mind the opportunity to use "warm vowels" on the word "Hallelujah" (ha-leh-loo-yah).

EXAMPLE 1: WORD EMPHASIS

EXAMPLE 2: ALTERNATE WORD EMPHASIS

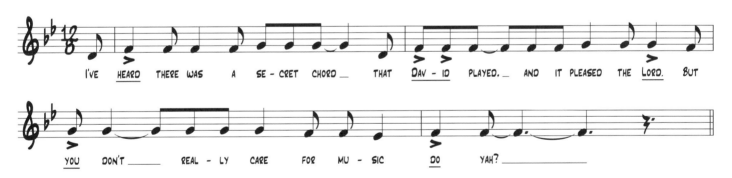

HALLELUJAH

Words and Music by
Leonard Cohen

HALLELUJAH

I've heard there was a secret chord

That David played, and it pleased the Lord.

But you don't really care for music do yah?

It goes like this, the fourth, the fifth,

The minor fall, the major lift;

The baffled king composing Hallelujah.

Hallelujah, hallelujah,

Hallelujah, hallelujah.

You say I took the name in vain

Though I don't even know the name.

But if I did, well really, what's it to yah?

There's a blaze of light in ev'ry word

It doesn't matter what you heard,

The holy or the broken Hallelujah.

Hallelujah, hallelujah,

Hallelujah, hallelujah.

I did my best, it wasn't much,

I couldn't feel so I tried to touch,

I've told the truth, I didn't come to fool yah.

And even though it all went wrong

I'll stand before the Lord of Song

With nothing on my tongue but Hallelujah.

Hallelujah, hallelujah,

Hallelujah, hallelujah.

Hallelujah, hallelujah,

Hallelujah, hallelujah.

FIELDS OF GOLD

FUN FACT:

"Fields of Gold" is one of Sting's most beautiful songs, but it failed to break the Billboard's Top 10 during its 1993 release. It went on to be covered by many artists, including Eva Cassidy. Few people are aware that Sting's given name is Gordon Sumner and he was an English major in college, and went on to teach it before making it big in music.

PERFORMANCE TIPS:

"Fields of Gold" is a ballad, and should be sung in a smooth and connected manner, which we call *legato*. Practice the exercises below. Make the words in example 2 sound just as smooth and connected as the "oo" warm vowel shape in example 1.

EXAMPLE 1: LEGATO SINGING WITH A VOWEL

EXAMPLE 2: LEGATO SINGING USING THE WORDS

More songs like this can be found in *Great Standards* Pro Vocal, Volume 22 (HL00740358).

FIELDS OF GOLD

Music and Lyrics by
Sting

Dolce (Sweetly) (♩ = 76)

[Sheet music notation]

Am   Am/G   Fmaj7   C(add9)/E   Dm7   Gsus   G   C(add9)   Am   Am/G

6 Fmaj7   C(add9)/E   Dm7   Gsus   G   C(add9)   Am   Am/G

YOU'LL RE - MEM - BER ME ___ WHEN THE

10 F(add9)   F   G7   C(add9)   Am   Am/G

WEST WIND MOVES ___ UP - ON THE FIELDS _ OF BAR - LEY. YOU'LL FOR - GET THE SUN ___ IN HIS

14 F(add9)   C(add9)/E   Dm7   G7   C   F/C   C   Am   Am/G

JEAL - OUS SKY ___ AS WE WALK IN FIELDS OF GOLD. SO SHE TOOK HER LOVE ___ FOR TO

18 F(add9)   F   G7   C(add9)   G/B   Am   Am/G

GAZE A WHILE ___ UP - ON THE FIELDS _ OF BAR - LEY. IN HIS ARMS SHE FELL ___ AS HER

22 F6/9   C(add9)/E   Dm7   Fmaj7   Gsus   G   C(add9)   Am   Am/G

HAIR CAME DOWN ___ A - MONG THE FIELDS OF GOLD. WILL YOU STAY WITH ME, ___ WILL YOU

26 F(add9)   G   C   G/B   Am7   G/B   C(add9)   C(add9)/E

BE MY LOVE ___ A - MONG THE FIELDS _ OF BAR - LEY? WE'LL FOR - GET THE SUN ___ IN HIS

30 F(add9)   G   C(add9)/E   Dm7   Fmaj7   Gsus   G   C(add9)   C/E   F(add9)

JEAL - OUS SKY ___ AS WE LIE IN FIELDS OF GOLD. I NEV - ER MADE

34 G(add9)   C(add9)   F(add9)   G(add9)   C(add9)   F(add9)

PROM - IS - ES LIGHT - LY, AND THERE HAVE BEEN SOME THAT I'VE BRO - KEN, BUT I SWEAR ___ IN THE

FIELDS OF GOLD

You'll remember me when the west wind moves

Upon the fields of barley.

You'll forget the sun in his jealous sky

As we walk in fields of gold.

So she took her love for to gaze a while

Upon the fields of barley.

In his arms she fell as her hair came down

Among the fields of gold.

Will you stay with me, will you be my love

Among the fields of barley?

We'll forget the sun in his jealous sky

As we lie in fields of gold.

I never made promises lightly,

And there have been some that I've broken,

But I swear in the days still left

We'll walk in fields of gold.

We will walk in fields of gold.

Many years have passed since those summer days

Among the fields of barley.

See the children run as the sun goes down

Among the fields of gold.

I never made promises lightly,

And there have been some that I've broken,

But I swear in the days still left

We'll walk in fields of gold.

We will walk in fields of gold.

You'll remember me when the west wind moves

Upon the fields of barley.

You can tell the sun in his jealous sky

When we walked in fields of gold,

When we walked in fields of gold.

FIRE AND RAIN

FUN FACTS:

James Taylor's iconic hit "Fire and Rain" contains the line "Sweet dreams and flying machines in pieces on the ground." Most people assume he was talking about a plane crash, but it was actually about the breakup of his recent band, The Flying Machine.

PERFORMANCE TIPS:

"Fire and Rain" is the perfect song to practice your "story telling" ability through song. Take time to recite the lyrics as if it were a poem, using typical vocal inflections and emphasis on important words and phrases. Now sing the song using that same intent on the lyrics. Tell the story!

In addition, watch for double vowels on "a" (eh-ee) and "I" (ah-ee) in the words "rain" and "fire." Always sing the first part of the vowel (eh or ah), before adding the (ee) only at the end of the word.

FIRE AND RAIN

Just yesterday morning, they let me know you were gone.

Suzanne, the plans they made put an end to you.

I walked out this morning and I wrote down this song.

Just can't remember who to send it to.

Oh, I've seen fire and I've seen rain.

I've seen sunny days that I thought would never end.

I've seen lonely times when I could not find a friend,

But I always thought that I'd see you again.

Won't you look down upon me, Jesus? You got to help me make a stand.

Just got to see me through another day.

My body's achin' and my time is at hand.

I won't make it any other way.

Whoa, I've seen fire and I've seen rain.

I've seen sunny days that I thought would never end.

I've seen lonely times when I could not find a friend,

But I always thought that I'd see you again.

Now I'm walking my mind to an easy time, my back turned towards the sun.

Lord knows when the cold wind blows it'll turn your head around.

Well, there's hours of time on the telephone line to talk about things to come:

Sweet dreams and flying machines in pieces on the ground.

Whoa, I've seen fire and I've seen rain.

I've seen sunny days that I thought would never end.

I've seen lonely times when I could not find a friend,

But I always thought that I'd see you again.

FIRE AND RAIN

Words and Music by
James Taylor

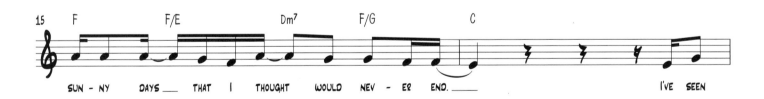

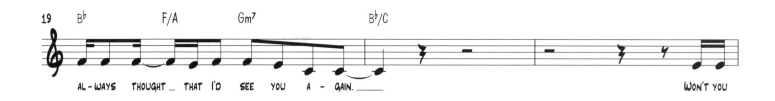

19

Bb · F/A · Gm7 · Bb/C

AL-WAYS THOUGHT _ THAT I'D SEE YOU A - GAIN. _____ WON'T YOU

22

C · Gm7 · F · C

LOOK DOWN UP-ON ME, JE - SUS? YOU GOT-TA HELP ME MAKE A STAND. _

24

G · Bbmaj7

YOU'VE JUST GOT TO SEE ME THROUGH AN-OTH - ER DAY.

26

C · Gm7 · F · C · G

MY BOD-Y'S ACH-ING AND MY TIME IS AT HAND ___ AND I WON'T MAKE IT AN-Y OTH-

29

Bbmaj7 · F · F/E · Dm7 · F/G · C

- ER WAY. WHOA. I'VE SEEN FIRE AND I'VE SEEN RAIN. ___ I'VE SEEN

32

F · F/E · Dm7 · F/G · C

SUN-NY DAYS ___ THAT I THOUGHT ___ WOULD NEV-ER END. ___ I'VE SEEN

34

F · F/E · Dm7 · F/G · C

LONE-LY TIMES ___ WHEN I COULD NOT FIND A FRIEND. ___ BUT I

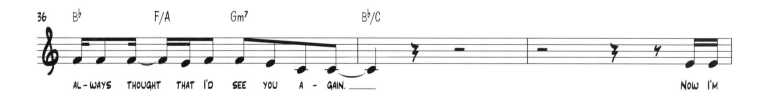

36

Bb · F/A · Gm7 · Bb/C

AL-WAYS THOUGHT THAT I'D SEE YOU A - GAIN. _____ NOW I'M

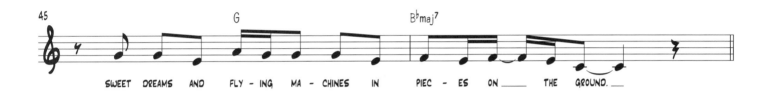

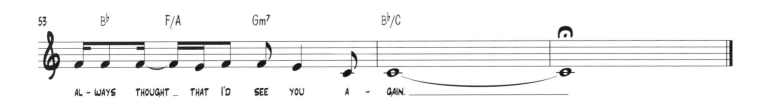

MAD WORLD

FUN FACT:

Mad World is a 1982 song by the British band Tears for Fears. It was written by Roland Orzabal but sung by the group's bassist, Curt Smith. Orzabal wrote the song on acoustic guitar while living above a pizza restaurant in the city of Bath, England, where he could look out onto the center of the city. "Not that Bath is very mad…I should have called it "Bourgeois World"!

PERFORMANCE TIPS:

A good way to add interest and drive to your singing is to slightly "rush up" the front side of each phrase and "slow down" the back side. For instance:

(Rush up) "All around me are familiar faces,

(Slow down) worn out places, worn out faces."

(Rush up) "Bright and early for their daily races,

(Slow down) going nowhere, going nowhere."

MAD WORLD

All around me are familiar faces, worn out places, worn out faces.

Bright and early for their daily races, going nowhere, going nowhere.

Their tears are filling up their glasses, no expression, no expression.

Hide my head, I wanna drown my sorrow, no tomorrow, no tomorrow.

And I find it kinda funny, I find it kinda sad

That dreams in which I'm dying are the best I've ever had.

I find it hard to tell you, I find it hard to take

When the people run in circles it's a very, very mad world. Mad world.

Children waiting for the day they feel good, happy birthday, happy birthday.

And I feel the way that every child should sit and listen, sit and listen.

Went to school and I was very nervous, no one knew me, no one knew me.

Hello teacher, tell me what's my lesson, look right through me, look right through me.

And I find it kinda funny, I find it kinda sad

That dreams in which I'm dying are the best I've ever had.

I find it hard to tell you, I find it hard to take

When the people run in circles it's a very, very mad world. Mad world.

Enlargen your world. Mad world.

MAD WORLD

Words and Music by
Roland Orzabal

SAD THAT DREAMS IN WHICH I'M DY-ING ARE THE BEST I'VE EV-ER HAD. I FIND IT HARD TO

TELL YOU. I FIND IT HARD TO TAKE WHEN PEO-PLE RUN IN CIR-CLES IT'S A VER-Y, VER-Y

MAD WORLD. ___ MAD WORLD. ___

EN-LARG-EN YOUR ___ WORLD. MAD WORLD. ___

HAVEN'T MET YOU YET

FUN FACTS:

Canadian-born Michael Bublé had a dream to be a professional singer from a very young age. In fact, his first album was entirely financed by himself. He was introduced to producer David Foster, who was reluctant to sign him to a record deal because he didn't know how to market his kind of music. He eventually signed Bublé…and the rest is history.

PERFORMANCE TIPS: ▶

Mature singers have three registers: chest (low notes), middle (mid-range notes), and head register (high notes). A great deal of pop music is sung in the chest and middle registers. The goal is to make them sound smooth and consistent. "Haven't Met You Yet" has a wide range that uses all three registers and will require expanding your range. Use the exercise below to help with that upper range. In addition, see the range extension exercise for "Crazy Little Thing Called Love" (page 59).

EXERCISE 1:

More songs like this can be found in *Michael Bublé Crazy Love* Pro Vocal, Volume 56 (HL00740439).

HAVEN'T MET YOU YET

I'm not surprised. Not ev'rything lasts.

I've broken my heart so many times, I stopped keepin' track.

Talk myself in, I talk myself out.

I get all worked up, then I let myself down.

I tried so very hard not to lose it.

I came up with a million excuses.

I thought I'd thought of ev'ry possibility.

And I know someday that it'll all turn out.

A-You'll make me work so we can work to work it out.

And I promise you, kid, that I'll give so much more
than I get.

I just haven't met you yet.

I might have to wait. I'll never give up.

I guess it's half timing, and the other half luck.

Wherever you are, whenever it's right,

You come out of nowhere and into my life.

And I know that we can be so amazin',

And baby, your love is gonna change me.

And now I can see ev'ry possibility.

And somehow I know that it'll all turn out,

And you'll make me work so we can work to work it out.

And I promise you, kid, I'll give so much more than I get.

I just haven't met you yet.

A-They say all's fair in love and war,

But I won't need to fight it.

We'll get it right and we'll be united.

And I know that we can be so amazin',

And bein' in your life is gonna change me.

And now I can see ev'ry single possibility,

And someday I know it'll all turn out,

And I'll work to work it out.

Promise you, kid, I'll give more than I get, than I get,
than I get, than I get.

Oh, you know it'll all turn out, and you'll make me work

So we can work to work it out.

And I promise you, kid, to give so much more
than I get, yeah.

I just haven't met you yet.

I just a-haven't met you yet.

Oh, I promise you, kid, to give so much more than I get.

I just haven't met you yet.

Ja, doi, day, ay, yeah.

I just haven't met you yet.

HAVEN'T MET YOU YET

Words and Music by Michael Bublé,
Alan Chang and Amy Foster

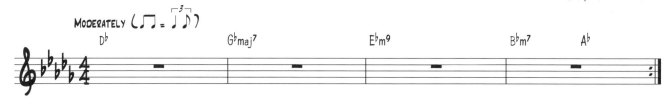

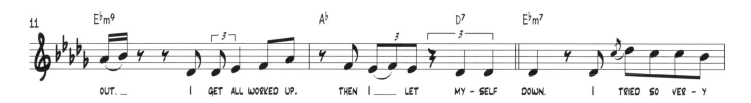

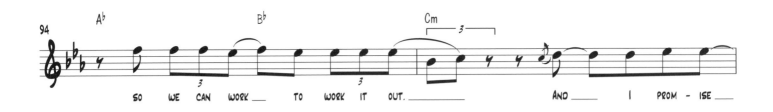

So we can work to work it out. And I prom - ise

you. Kid. to give so much more than I get. Yeah. I

just have - n't met you yet.

I just a - have - n't met you yet. Oh, I

prom - ise you. Kid. to give so much more than I get.

Just have - n't met you yet. Ja, doi, day, ay,

yeah. I just have - n't met you yet.

PERFECT

FUN FACTS:

Ed Sheeran built his fan base via YouTube with his own self-produced recordings for several years before being picked up and distributed through a record label.

PERFORMANCE TIPS:

Enunciation is important to communicating the words of your song to an audience. "Perfect" is an excellent opportunity to use crisp consonants. Remember "The lips, the teeth, the tip of the tongue" exercise? Below is another excellent exercise for building your articulators. Practice it and then apply the concept to the lyrics of the song.

EXERCISE 1:

SIT ON A PO - TA - TO PAN, O - TIS!   SIT ON A PO - TA - TO PAN, O - TIS!*

* A PALINDROME... THE SAME PHRASE FORWARD AND BACKWARD!

More songs like this can be found in *Ed Sheeran Music Minus One Vocals* (HL00275772).

PERFECT

I found a love for me.

Darling, just dive right in, follow my lead.

Well, I found a girl, beautiful and sweet.

Well, I never knew you were the someone waiting for me.

'Cause we were just kids when we fell in love,

Not knowing what it was.

I will not give you up this time.

Darling, just kiss me slow,

Your heart is all I own.

And in your eyes, you're holding mine.

Baby, I'm dancing in the dark

With you between my arms.

Barefoot on the grass,

Listening to our fav'rite song.

When you said you looked a mess,

I whispered underneath my breath.

But you heard it, "Darling, you look perfect tonight."

Well, I found a woman, stronger than anyone I know.

She shares my dreams, I hope that someday,
I'll share her home.

I found a love to carry more than just my secrets,

To carry love, to carry children of our own.

We are still kids but we're so in love,

Fighting against all odds.

I know we'll be alright this time.

Darling, just hold my hand.

Be my girl, I'll be your man.

I've seen my future in your eyes.

Baby, I'm dancing in the dark

With you between my arms.

Barefoot on the grass,

Listening to our fav'rite song.

When I saw you in that dress,

Looking so beautiful, I don't deserve this.

"Darling, you look perfect tonight."

Baby, I'm dancing in the dark

With you between my arms.

Barefoot on the grass,

Listening to our fav'rite song.

I have faith in what I see,

Now I know I have met an angel in person

And she looks perfect.

I don't deserve this, you look perfect tonight.

PERFECT

Words and Music by
Ed Sheeran

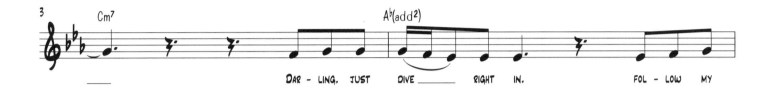

32 Eb(add2)　　　　　　　　　　　　　　　　　　Cm7

TO CAR - RY MORE THAN JUST MY SE - CRETS. TO CAR - RY

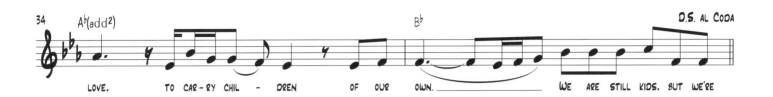

34 Ab(add2)　　　　　　　　　　　　　　Bb　　　　　　　　D.S. AL CODA

LOVE. TO CAR-RY CHIL - DREN OF OUR OWN. _____ WE ARE STILL KIDS, BUT WE'RE

CODA
　Eb　　　　　Bb　　　　　Eb　　　　　　　　　　　　**2**

YOU LOOK PER - FECT TO-NIGHT."

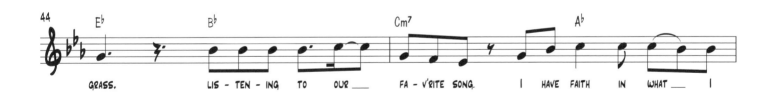

40 Bb　　　　　　　　　　　　　　Cm7　　　　　　Abmaj9

BA - BY, _____ I'M _____ DANC - ING IN THE

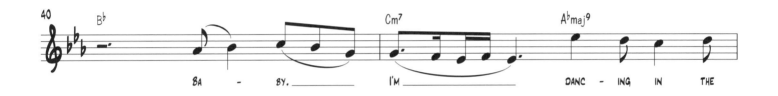

42 Eb　　　　　　　Bb　　　　　　　　Cm7　　　　　Abmaj9

DARK WITH YOU BE - TWEEN MY ARMS. BARE - FOOT ON THE

44 Eb　　　　　Bb　　　　　　　　　Cm7　　　　　　Ab

GRASS. LIS - TEN-ING TO OUR ___ FA - V'RITE SONG. I HAVE FAITH IN WHAT ___ I

46 Eb　　　　　Bb　　　　　Cm7　　　　　Ab　　　　　Eb　　　　　Bb

SEE. NOW I KNOW I HAVE MET AN AN - GEL IN PER - SON AND SHE LOOKS PER - FECT. I

49 Absus2　　　　　　　　　　　Bb　　　　　　　**2**

DON'T DE - SERVE THIS. YOU LOOK PER - FECT TO-NIGHT.

YESTERDAY

FUN FACTS:

The original lyrics to "Yesterday" were "Scrambled Eggs!" Often songwriters use "dummy" lyrics temporarily while songwriting and then revise them after the fact.

PERFORMANCE TIPS:

Vibrato is a musical effect consisting of a regular, pulsating change of pitch. It is used to add expression to vocal and instrumental music. Most popular singing uses very little vibrato. However, there are two types to be aware of, which are demonstrated in examples 2 and 3 below. "Yesterday," like most ballads, presents an excellent opportunity to use vibrato to add expression to the song.

EXAMPLE 1: STRAIGHT, NO VIBRATO

EXAMPLE 2: STRAIGHT TONE TO VIBRATO

EXAMPLE 3: DIRECTLY TO VIBRATO

More songs like this can be found in *The Beatles Music Minus One Vocals* (HL00236167).

YESTERDAY

Yesterday, all my troubles seemed so far away.

Now it looks as though they're here to stay.

Oh, I believe in yesterday.

Suddenly, I'm not half the man I used to be.

There's a shadow hangin' over me.

Oh, yesterday came suddenly.

Why she had to go, I don't know, she wouldn't say.

I said something wrong, now I long for yesterday.

Yesterday, love was such an easy game to play.

Now I need a place to hide away.

Oh, I believe in yesterday.

Why she had to go, I don't know, she wouldn't say.

I said something wrong, now I long for yesterday.

Yesterday, love was such an easy game to play.

Now I need a place to hide away.

Oh, I believe in yesterday.

Yesterday

Words and Music by John Lennon
and Paul McCartney

Moderately

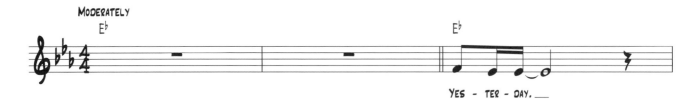

YES - TER - DAY. ___

ALL MY TROU - BLES SEEMED SO FAR A - WAY. ___

NOW IT LOOKS ___ AS THOUGH ___ THEY'RE HERE TO STAY. ___ OH,

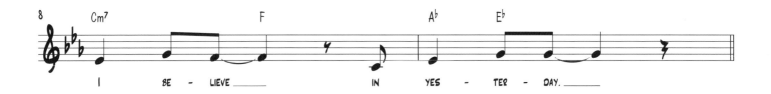

I BE - LIEVE ___ IN YES - TER - DAY. ___

SUD - DEN - LY. ___ I'M NOT HALF THE MAN ___ I

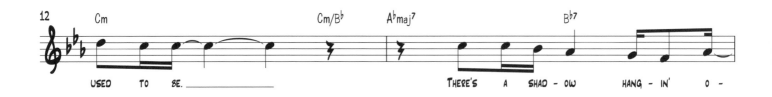

USED TO BE. ___ THERE'S A SHAD - OW HANG - IN' O -

- VER ME. ___ OH, YES - TER - DAY ___ CAME

39   E♭   E♭   Dm   G7

DAY. _____   YES - TER - DAY, _____   LOVE WAS SUCH AN EAS - Y

42   Cm   Cm/B♭   A♭maj7   B♭7

GAME   TO   PLAY. _____   NOW   I   NEED _____ A   PLACE _____ TO

44   E♭   E♭/D   Cm7   F

HIDE   A - WAY. _____   OH,   I   BE - LIEVE _____   IN

46   A♭   E♭   E♭/B♭   F7/A   A♭   E♭

                                    RIT.

YES - TER - DAY. _____   MM. _____

CRAZY LITTLE THING CALLED LOVE

FUN FACTS:

"Crazy Little Thing Called Love" was Queen's first number one hit. Written by Freddie Mercury and released in 1980, it featured him playing rhythm guitar, which was quite rare, and was the first time he played it on stage with Queen.

PERFORMANCE TIPS:

This song is best suited for tenors or high baritones because of its higher notes. The exercise below will help you build and extend your upper range of notes. The online audio features *PLAYBACK+* which allows you to lower the key for greater vocal comfort.

EXERCISE 1:

More songs like this can be found in *Queen* Pro Vocal Volume 15 (HL00740453).

CRAZY LITTLE THING CALLED LOVE

Words and Music by
Freddie Mercury

Moderately Fast Swing

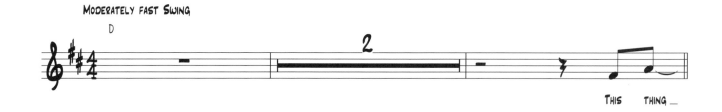

This thing ___

___ called love. ___ I just ___ can't han - dle it. ___ This thing ___

___ called love. ___ I ___ must ___ get 'round

___ to it. ___ I ain't read - y, Cra - zy lit - tle thing called love. ___

___ Uh, this thing _____ called love. ___

___ It ___ cries ___ in a cra - dle all night. ___ It swings. ___

CRAZY LITTLE THING CALLED LOVE

This thing called love, I just can't handle it.

This thing called love, I must get 'round to it.

I ain't ready, crazy little thing called love.

Uh, this thing called love, it cries in a cradle all night.

It swings, it jives, it shakes all over like a jellyfish.

I kinda like it, crazy little thing called love.

There goes my baby, she knows how to rock and roll.

She drives me crazy, she gives me hot and cold fever,

Then she leaves me in a cool, cool sweat.

I gotta be cool, relax, get hip, get on my tracks.

Take a back seat, hitchhike, and take a long ride on the motorbike

Until I'm ready, crazy little thing called love.

I gotta be cool, relax, get hip, get on my tracks.

Take a back seat, hitchhike, and take a long ride on my motorbike

Until I'm ready, crazy little thing called love.

This thing called love, I just can't handle it.

This thing called love, I must get 'round to it.

I ain't ready, crazy little thing called love,

Crazy little thing called love. *(sing 7 times)*